Vanishing-Line

Books by Jeffrey Yang

Poetry

An Aquarium
Vanishing-Line

Translation

East Slope by Su Shi
June Fourth Elegies by Liu Xiaobo

Editor

Birds, Beasts, and Seas: Nature Poems from New Directions
Two Lines: Some Kind of Beautiful Signal (with Natasha Wimmer)

Vanishing-Line

POEMS

Jeffrey Yang

GRAYWOLF PRESS

This publication is made possible by funding provided in part by a grant from the Minnesota State Arts Board, through an appropriation by the Minnesota State Legislature, a grant from the National Endowment for the Arts, and private funders. Significant support has also been provided by Target; the McKnight Foundation; and other generous contributions from foundations, corporations, and individuals. To these organizations and individuals we offer our heartfelt thanks.

Thanks to the editors involved in the following publications for first publishing some of these poems: Gerald Maa and Lawrence Minh-Davis at the *Asian American Literary Review*; Quincy Troupe at *Black Renaissance/Renaissance Noire*; Robert N. Casper et al. at *jubilat*; Katie Raissian and Anna Della Subin at *Stonecutter*; Ben Fama and Michael Barron at *Supermachine*; Chris Caldemeyer et al. at *Washington Square Review: 26*; David Lau and Calvin Bedient at *Lana Turner*; and Christopher Mattison and Roland Pease at *Zoland Poetry*.

Published by Graywolf Press
250 Third Avenue North, Suite 600
Minneapolis, Minnesota 55401

www.graywolfpress.org

Published in the United States of America

ISBN 978-1-55597-594-4

2 4 6 8 9 7 5 3 1
First Graywolf Printing, 2011

Library of Congress Control Number: 2011930482

Cover design: Jeenee Lee

Cover art: Mu Xin, *Dawn Mood at Bohai*, detail. Yale University Art Gallery. Gift of the Rosenkranz Charitable Foundation at the request of Alexandra Munroe and Robert Rosenkranz, B. A. 1962.

for 爸爸 (1931–1996)
for my mother and sister

and for Michelle, Arjun, and Qingxi

Contents

A thought which can be called a thought of recognition because it traces the vanishing-line of the times ...

—ALEXANDER GARCÍA DÜTTMANN

Vanishing-Line

Place

        to perceive
a voice in the storm

unwanted voice
away from home

       wave-break

vessel on vessel
floating

clouds   clear   wind

starboard waves, no,
whales approach

Throne

Have the poets left anywhere
in need of patching? Or did you,
after imaginings,
recognize her abode?

—'ANTARA, 6TH CENTURY

out of the dragon's mouth
freed from the body of death
in the grave in the sea

cast out a fool, mere
shadow   puppet

twice dead, son
of the widow of Zarephath
Elijah's resurrected

city we would raze any-
way over and again

Medes, Babylonians

lines burying lines
of our existence

~

or was it Sin
of the moon
in his brothers' place

on the hissarlik mound
bound by Tigris and Khosr

who changed the river's course
for the palace on Kuyunjik

city of 18 gates slaves built

for his glory, Assur's,
forms center and boundary

two hundred years later its
ancient name buried

Xenophon passing thru thought:
"Achaemenids destroyed this Medean city"

~

the actual dispersed
in memories, legends
and their exegesis, geographers
or travelers, fragmented
in earth annals, curls
of a beard, palm's shade
fish cloak, apkallu winged
sage, guardian spirits
scarab seal

foundation deposits
undeciphered till the 1850s

while the pillage continues

vaults lean against throne for profit
avarice off the gold-standard

~

what Rawlinson Westmacott missed, beauty
other than the Elgin marbles

strange beauty in the service of power
a renaissance

Of Medici Angelico magi

Sassetti's books plated
à mon pouvoir ... à mon pouvoir ...

omers of wine
omers of first fruits

cedar   pine   cypress
carried from snow-capped
Amanus, Baltai quarry
a divine revelation

Mosul marble alabaster
mottled barley of Mt. Nipur,

Kapridargilâ breccia, giš-
nugallu of Mt. Ammanana

presiding colossi, winged
bull winged lion with
human heads

"as the bombs fell
I ran thru the streets
watching the bombs fall on TV"

～

carved on throne-room walls:

I besieged, I conquered,
I carried off the spoils

armory making peace
relative to power

walked upon a river
fish swimming inside

Michael, how your lines surfaced
The lines through these words

form other, still longer lines

~

Izdubar begins empire

and the banks a deluge of accounts

poor commodities to depend upon
forever unsettled, farmed humanity

at the heart of history
generations forced
into wilderness
camps, unable to wander

that a world without guns
would be a world without eternity

power in the throne-room suite
dispersed tragedy

~

library tablet found underground:

dove sent forth returned
swallow sent forth returned
raven sent forth saw corpses
it ate, then wandered away

animals sent forth to the four winds
I poured a libation, built an altar
on a mountain peak, cut seven herbs
placed reeds, pines, sigmar beneath

the gods gathered at the burning
the gods gathered at the good burning
the gods gathered like flies over the sacrifice

~

define the four quarters of the earth
as the Zagros mountains east and north
arid plains south, west further

to sea

kings trace past the 21st century BC
time's mirror sorrow

mirage of space and boundary

he proceeded "to break down
every wall that seemed likely to contain
relics of the past"

scattered to the highest bidder

~

are those lotus blossoms
patterning the pavement

and the walls of gazelles and onagers
urdimmu the lion-legged, eagle-
footed djinn

prisoners and deportees
conifers and grapevines

in a river valley between wooded mountains
water sweeps waste heaps

"conquest of my hands"

not a window but a field

~

wall after wall of conquest

power's assurance, tradition
of self-glory

temporal record spread
thru the halls, publicity
peace thru the threat of war

laborers in turbans with earflaps
tall headdresses of Phoenician women

captives in animal skins
spoils in transport, foodbearers

carry the baskets, mold the bricks
slabs sledge hauls with ropes

horsemen and charioteers
archers at siege at siege

gateway bull:
"From the upper sea of the setting sun . . .
to the lower sea of the rising sun . . .
made all the rulers of the world
bow down at my feet"

tribute from Hezekiah of Judah

~

"pious shepherd, fearful of the great gods"
translated to
"expert shepherd, favorite of the great gods"

along with new bronze casts
calmed the waters
with canebrake swamps

built aqueducts, canals
orchards watered in summer
in winter a thousand fields

planted a cylinder
of words

prism   of words

language
disintegrates
like a crystal throne

the pen moves without
the hand knowing

~

rose

leaves on a tomb

foster favorable circumstances
and your inclinations will bloom

~

temple ziggurat base built over
to whom do we pray to

ladder or shield

Ishtar, daughter of Sin
or Hea, of the flood of the sea

Herodotus:
"The shrine contains no image,
and no one spends the night there except
(if we are to believe the Chaldeans
who are the priests of Bel) one
Assyrian woman, all alone,
whoever it may be
that the god has chosen"

~

by the river

in Nineveh, Austen Henry Layard, 1840:

"The site was covered with grass and flowers, and
the enclosure, formed by the long line of mounds
which marked the ancient walls of the city, afforded
pasture to the flocks of a few poor Arabs who had
pitched their black tents within it. There was at that
time nothing to indicate the existence of the splendid
remains of Assyrian palaces which were covered by
the heaps of earth and rubbish. It was believed that the
great edifices and monuments . . . had perished with
her people, and like them had left no wreck behind."

~

across the river

E. L. Mitford, 1840:

"Mosul is an ill-constructed mud-built town, ris-
ing above the banks of the Tigris, and backed by low
hills; in the centre is a tall brown ugly minaret, very
much out of the perpendicular; the interior of some
of the houses is faced with a translucent stone, called
Mosul marble. . . . Part of the old Saracen walls still
remain: they are very massive . . . the ground be-
tween the walls and the town is occupied by stag-
nant pools, ruins and dead bodies of camels and
cattle, which is enough to breed a pestilence; the ba-
zaars are mean and dirty."

~

downriver

to Baghdad, George Smith, 1873:

"The city is large and principally built on the east-
ern bank of the Tigris; there are many fine buildings
and large bazaars, and outside the town there are miles
of gardens and abundance of productions. From
my window in the Residency I enjoyed a charm-
ing prospect; immediately in front was a plantation
with orange trees, vines, and sweet-smelling plants,
beyond this a splendid view of the river Tigris then
in flood, and on the other side of the water a grove of
palm trees with a primitive Arab machine for raising
water from the river to irrigate the ground."

~

at the river

in Baghdad, Gertrude Bell, December 7, 1917:

"The new régime promises well. I haven't seen
General Marshall since I came back but he gives
signs of being sympathetic towards our side of the
game. It's as well, for we were running fast on to
rocks, in my opinion . . . The presence of an enemy
is an essential element in battle. And we can't walk
after him indefinitely because an army walks on its
stomach. Vigorous steps have been taken to ensure
a good harvest next spring—but that is not till the
middle of April and meantime we are going to be
hard put to it to get the civil population fed."

September 5, 1920:

"Over and over again people have said to me that it has been a shock and a surprise to them to see Europe relapse into barbarism. I had no reply—what else can you call the war? How can we, who have managed our own affairs so badly, claim to teach others to manage theirs better? It may be that the world has need to sink back into the dark ages of chaos, out of which it will evolve something, perhaps no better than what it had."

January 16, 1923:

"I don't feel reasonable myself—how can one when political values are as fluctuating as the currency? At the back of my mind I have a feeling that we people of the war can never return to complete sanity. The shock has been too great; we're unbalanced. . . . Niffar is by far the most striking site I've seen here . . . you see in section age after age of civilization extending over a period of three or four thousand years. It's amazing and rather horrible to be brought face to face with millenniums of human effort and then to consider what a mess we've made of it."

~

king falls to bishop

bishop falls to caliph
caliph falls to khan
khan to sultan to sheikh
to prime minister regent colonel brig-
adier general president

these the descendents of power
that vanish with place

tho not the place
in people, who live
with the scattering
invisible to history, inevitably
transformed

~

in accord with the ancient books
and the traditions of the past

the monks called it Samarra,
city of Shem, eldest son of Noah,

and al-Mu'tasim, eighth Abbasid Caliph,
bought the fertile land from the monks
for his Turkish army, al-Mas'udi tells us,

then some twenty years later, al-
Mutawakkil built a palace there

its design an army drawn
in battle lines, the two wings
right and left flanks connected
by army center portico

as the Nu'man king had constructed it
in Hira [before Arabic, liturgy sung
in Syriac] for "he had a passion for war . . .
wishing always to have it constantly in mind"

this Nestorian palace cast in the mosaics
of the Umayyad mosque in Damascus

~

al-Mas'udi 943 recognizes the ruins
surrounding the villages and farms

Ibn Battuta in the fourteenth century
sees the hill of Nabi Yunus
a spring of the same name
the remains of the encircling walls
and the position of the gates

today, three weeks before Lent, residents
still observe the Fast of the Ninevites

~

at the threshold
in the margin

of the line

thought's spine

down the ladder leaves and
flowers

surrounds
the seat of power

circles time

underground, un-
to
fire and earth-
bound

water, seeps

memory, mercury
vapor

forming sun
nearest to sun

birth happiness

~

kikiun withers, death
be swift, worm's eye

pen, ark of screen
sun burning down

blind as sand, reason

~

pellitory-of-the-wall perilla pelagios
torii knell doubling the dead

toward what end if any
from belly borne, for

what anger, angel descended
to have served the story

myth of solace

the child in happiness
anticipates answering, *I am*

the one who accompanies
the poem, sings the child-king

from the other side of death

~

wynde-hidden words
there the island, there the sea

floating island mass of the mind
vanishing beyond vanishing-line

Lyric Suite

Away in the loveable west,
On a pastoral forehead of Wales,
I was under a roof here, I was at rest,
And they the prey of the gales;

—G. M. HOPKINS

Trees turned to branches
yellow leaves all around

the city, rain-
fall

Elder one leaving

the corner for
the road

        behind

memory

        ~

Past remembering
        the past disappears

snowed city, old
concealed

Frozen river

Bird tracks thru the trees

someone's speaking
"see you soon . . . I love you"

        ~

strange code

being old
far from friends
home

tongue turns
to stone

~

For years she passed
between six children
grown

distant
　　　　land
where the heart began

~

Water-color-by numbers

Brush her hair in front of the mirror

If you knew the end would near like this

among strangers
sitting by a television
in a clean, warm
place, nowhere

Where the mind
goes, what it leaves behind in its absence

until your ashes returned home

~

Everything near becomes distant
Goethe says of twilight, Borges
of blindness, past to self
self to others, within us
we live by an invisible Sun
that burns with timelessness
dust of the sky, clarity
of distance

~

closer to earth
another birth, prospect
of equality

~

War rained

notes from planes

She put her dowry to paper, people
read: *the Emperor's dead*

Wedding bands donated
to the soldiers' Winter Clothing Campaign

Things unreal she never spoke of
filtered thru family memory

On the run husband kidnapped, jailed, she freed

He had a lover, but she never left him
nor he her

fury, I too young to see before his death

～

Her father

in a temple body left

never buried never burned
by those who loved

him, lost

to them, who saw him
last?

Family dispersed
Some fled to an island
with the promise of return

～

Her mother in urn island ossuary

Digital chants, red bulbs, incense,
certain flies nameless visitors

~

Of the party served
in a community of resistance

That the party she served
purged, mass-
murdered, colonized, displaced

How-much-known-or-not-known
matters
of the original good

for power, embattled
drift

Her children
she preserved

~

Constant migrations
city to city

Salt an economy

devil
erased the details

same devil
that created the Chinese language
as St. Guthlac heard in the Crowland fens

Island's original inhabitants erased
Atayal genocide

Native story

to adapt the lifeways
and stay annihilation

~

Yami Island
off Pakan

Party turned into prison

Fish cannery actually
nuclear waste dump
10,000-year-half-life

Today children still-
born

~

The story of this past
is one of great and unexpected changes,
stops and starts, abrupt shifts and reversals
Segrè writes of Earth's
temporal evolution

~

west of rest is sleep
east, dream
where waters meet
north, emptiness,
south, wakefulness,
and out, rising up
to the stars, peace

~

rock
compressed into diamond
thru mine-
distance touched
by that shining
prism, fragments
lost ground
to dust

~

Too easy to imagine
her life, fill in the facts
with birds
in a burning palm
what are they doing
plucking culls
from the burning crown
while ripened fruit
surrounds them

Miserable facts
hollow shells found
in a dune

Dunes I walked
of a different island,
wind-scorched sands
holding secrets
of ancient birds
and shells, empty
metal shells rusted
silence

~

hermit crab
scurries and grows
into its new home
like a pre-
historic materialist
with new needs

~

I was a child when I walked with her
thru the lattice streets of the island
feeling lost but safe
with her, the most foreign
element of the city this belongingness
crowded together public
space, streets where people
read and cooked, played
chess, elders watched children,
commerce spilled into
conversation, her
neighborhood at the city's
brink, industry, lifeless river
weight of humidity, of memory

~

Thru the window

swimming pool (she walked
slowly round and round
head down)

eucalyptus
owl gone, slope
to canyon coyotes
gone

Valley
lake edge dried to desert,
tilled for irises, turned to
sprinklered links water-
trap birds

Beside a vineyard
new house tracts
lawn to lawn cul-de-sacs
where children play
with their class, a suburb

once a ranch

　　　foal belly yellow
　　　under mother

and the hidden fields around
a miracle of the immigrants

Thru the limits of alternatives
she looked out
at rice rain

　　～

all that converges
along the vanishing-line
opens out exponentially

　　～

When her first-
born son died
no one told her

What she knew:
silence

The silence
of an empty bridge
in a dream
where I meet my father

~

Adagio appassionato
of Berg's unsymphony
Sun stretto shadows
lengthening strings, poco
a poco ritardando
scenes, time ceases to be
more than tempo, molto
tranquillo mind
ceases to be
more than memory, brief
arpeggio, calando legatissimo, ever
fainter echo pianissimo, farewell
measure, farewell
twilight, farewell
blindness, farewell distant
melody

~

Children, when they are born,
and old people, when they die,
don't talk, they see something.
                        —J.-L. GODARD

~

Nine-dragon wine set
gift from her father

The Treasure of China
gift from generalissimo Jiang

Silver phoenix bracelet embraces
double leaves and flowers
sent from her husband during the war
with a green-bamboo silk fan

—lone traveler by a lake
brushed with the words:
life's true joy   belongs to a fisherman

~

On West Lake she boats
childhood summer wind
endless
   radiance
Fold upon fold
of lotus-
bloom water
    circling Sun

in memory of 魏慶安
Wei Qing An (1907–2003)

36

Two Spanish Poems

I. Hamra Hissarlik

Carmen walled garden
walk thru Nazarí needle:

Fountain
        'carved
as a shell'

in the Patio del
Cuarto Dorado

Muhammed's design
arrow-sheaf yoked
by the monarchs

Open sky inside
sun slants
down
      walls
divided shadow
and light

Law's solemnity

to embody justice
thru us

abandoned
with drone civility

The wealth
of our desolation,
      the vanity
of a nation

Memory upon memory of stone

wood, tapia, stucco,
          linked star dado,
spandrels lead to frieze

each form
follows its intention,
          each carving
a hidden glory

curved soffit, jarred niches

          not figurative
but the immanence
of the Sacred Table

Floral kufic, chamfered letters

epigraphic arabesques wall
to wall

wa la ghalib ill Allah
wa la ghalib ill Allah

and the liturgy overlayed
by morisco crafstmen

          At the outer rampart
of the Puerta de la Justicia,

the hand in the keystone
of the heart
bears the five precepts

By the light of the court

water-channel paths, body

mostly water,
        balanced
in temperature and quantity

for us to survive the centuries
spirit thirsts

Before the Comares façade
choose:

one door to the public
one door to the private

Mocárabes tariqa radiates
Allah's stars

down to the lower lamps
tarima sleep

Tourists' happiness:
to leave, to return

Where paths converge up watersteps
beneath a pergola of laurel to the mirador

overlooking civilization

II. An Archaeology

onyx light
travertine, green
marble walls

roof flat rectangle
water

wall
    of glass
shades

air
simple as sorrow

spare chromium frame columns

stone grain

rough white wall
turns a corner and ends
for waterscape

shallow pool with rocks
each rock clear, a clear
crowd of rocks

a pavilion for warm weather

Barcelona

chairs in a doorless
room, glass

mullion window
panels floor to ceiling, anti-
exedra

glabrous stone, russet
reds

time's compression, apparent

pieced together
with simple precision

exacting
but demands nothing

ornament's absence

on a raised stone slab with brief
steps to connect
earth

stone steps
a man sits on
to collect a fee

he could be a thief
no one around

far into the mechanical age
fraction of a fossil's age

another arrives and hesitantly pays
then says he's been cheated

nothing to see, the cost
of nothing

immanent remains

or maybe the
'imminence of a revelation
which does not occur'

roofless walls
glass planes grey, white,
green, clear
reflections

translucent transience

space
        for air

another pool of still water
smaller, surrounded by olivine
mineral elements, marble

walls and roof shape
water
rectangle
        of sky

Kolbe's Morning granite
nude in the water she
gazes into

her head turns slightly
to the side and down

her arms curve overhead, one
stretches forward, away, hand
pushes up
in front of the other
hand fans
down

a bud opening, her eyes
prepare for light

legs and feet together, slight
knee-bend, feet tilt
flat on a stone slant
dance

she doesn't belong here
her curves, her craft
literal, she is
trapped

at the other end a small gift shop
room
ridiculous flag poles

this place
not exactly luxury, not
exactly built

cut, sanded, polished

balanced, tensionless

human tools

lines follow
rock
meets steel, meets glass

water

as if it's always existed
any-
where
for us to find

and recognize where

wall ends

a black cat reclines
on the rough white stone
sun, tail-
flick

line of stone benches
M. and I sit, lean
hand in hand against
wall, sun-

light
blinds us with
reflecting white
waterscape

bright
parrot shapes
flap in the grassy distance

Tide Table

"A child drowned in the sea.
So a cow was driven into the waves
and made to swim out to sea"

We were watching
but couldn't see

Suffering traced to suffering's release

Charcoal cliffs, sea
shore tide
calm

Clouds in
waves
erasing waves

beach chairs bungalows   waves
break, breaking
                  wave
after wave

of memory

In a room

on a wall projection
of a projection

Cow's eye

dreaming
eye of the
          cloud
in the wave in the
man

looking out from a hotel balcony

plump white pinstriped
he reads the newspaper
cameo zoom, Tide Table
graph pan,

          man's
feet flow

"Provisional Purchase"
"Minimal Indolence"
"Sale in Execution"

the metaphysic
of commodity exchange: to never know
          with whom we're connected

The man falls asleep
in beach chair
face under broadsheet
Ngana adagio dirge
begins

African woman hums lullaby

lines turn things alive:
a chair dances, another breaks

But as soon as it emerges as a commodity,
it changes into a thing which transcends sensuousness.
It not only stands with its feet on the ground, but,
in relation to all other commodities, it stands on its head,
and evolves out of its wooden brain grotesque ideas,
far more wonderful than if it began dancing of its own
free will

Indoor shower droplets
morph into cows
drown, slaughtered
hung on hooks
by an invisible hand
More cows materialize
at sea, thin
carcasses wash ashore

Kaufmann's reverse-time-lapse
diagonal metamorphoses filmed

      In a dream

of capital
as source of social relation
organization

Knife inscribed circa 8th century BC:
Everlasting legal money of Qi
at the Establishment of the State

The woman watches over a boy

who builds a sandcastle
pushes a friend in a wheelbarrow
throws a stone into sea

Between man and boy
self, between
                tide
pattern and dream

One line vanishes, another appears

Lone lightbulb, hanging
buckets, sand-
bucket military base

Two children play in the waves
chair skips, collapses round bucket
waves, shack glows
inside with tide in which
a figure dances

shore outside

he hops
        on
            sea-
rocks

Lightbulb rays line-swirl chair
becomes bed

Three officers survey beach
from binocular balcony, sky
darkens, cows
decompose to bones

Pharaoh's dream
bolex camera frame
to frame
erased

a dream of abundance followed by drought

Man alone
on beach asleep

Existence as much emptiness
as motion

man and child
erasing each other

Hospital beds accumulate
in bungalow shacks, sickness
overflows

patients piled onto wheel-
barrow

Baptismal procession choir
cross and star of david

Financial pages fly beneath
walking feet, paper
paves the way she
walks, pages blow
away

death claims
one without hospital

Wheelbarrow memorial, body
taken to tide another holds
in surf
            water
rises, recedes
shrouds vanish beneath

Bystander . . . bystander
to be baptized
is to perceive more
than one sees

Gold
credit
        crisis
to crisis collapse:

money materializes
half the world   still
starves

Forgotten images, thoughts
of recognition

Enclosed room

The man wakes

behind binocular
blink
eyes, beach
tide rhythm

casts a stone into sea

Light floods the screen

the bright
white light

of interrogation

Elegy for Ling　靈　灵

spirit consumed by fire
shaman warps to pig's head
rain above open mouths
doorway
between shaman and rainfall

ling heart-
tone
of the temple gate
of the zero-moon

echo of jade brilliance
red phosphorous spirit
        spirit
of being un-
making *ling*

soul dim light flit-
ting
eaves splitting maborosi light will-
o'-the-wisp
drawing her nearer

across
what distances
                darknesses

ling

beyond the waste mountains
water stream-
ing stones
            that
sound of

water against stones
of jade pendants
of bells
of antelope horns among branches
of damask
of feathers of
the creaking wheel
ling
unrecognizable behind the lattice
pages and pages float-
ing down

scales
scars tearing apart, heart
sliver of light ice prison

to the measured position

of the cracking entablature
at the architrave's cusp
crumbling beneath her

ling
looking down

on the ruined city of her birth
facing

the unravelling

the expanding the contracting
the pull of the end

that night before the wedding
before her arrival

where were you ling
sewing the wedding dress

sewing the seconds

her little brother before her

the boy who jumped thru the atrium
the boy with the gun, the boy who drowned

old men sorting thru rubble, brick by brick
rebuilding the ancient walls
while the ring roads expand
while the machinery explodes
the celebrity architects multiply
ignorant of the original design

coal in the lungs sand in the lungs
carbon monoxide poly-
chlorinated biphenyl red
dust in the lungs

the hanged woman's house sold
her belongings sold windows barred
tree cursed

the man on his bicycle hit by a train

it was pouring rain

on the forest on the thorptops

that night before the wedding
before her arrival

ancient observatory
wrapped between highways
between hotels and satellite dishes
billboards and metal cranes
       at the intersection
daoists buddhists muslims
weighing the heavens, watching
with bronze instruments on a roof of stone
before the jesuits, before verbiest's refitting
his *ruder muse,* before stumpf's melting of the yuan
3300 years ago a nova guest star recorded on an oracle bone
now gaseous haze for sky
electricity spinning arenaceous air
drowning perception
of the forged inventions
armillary spheres
red road equatorial *yellow road* ecliptic
quadrant sextant celestial globe
polar axis spins positioning the stars
dragon theodolite azimuth theodolite

at theta at teth at sun at death

like drowning in open ocean, I.C. wrote

the map was there, her laugh is there
alone with the signs

the patterns the biochemicals
the codons the proteins

translating un-
folding

the final despair of the final decision
eyes clear eyes bright
to the received translation

ling
cipher spirit-source

ling
mystical deer mystical fish
anteater wagtail dace

ling
Libellulidae winging water
    chestnut
    fall-
ing
       rain

thru the threshold
of the mind

of the wine
of the sill
of the thin stone port-
hole boat bottle with handle
tilling channel accumulating
ice

ling
tomb plume mound coffin

yin of the *wu*-shaman
Quercus on Sumeru

lonely lake wound-
ing light

traversing the lintel

for us left
the looking forward looking back
at the bridge at the river

without reconciliation without expiation
sound breaking clear

ing

eyes of turquoise and coral
cannot see

motherless children
love's innocence

    children

on the stairs

Yennecott

Me, earthdweller, with the wave
Of one foot breaking
After another

(V. K.)

~

Off the main road
thru a tangled path of green
to a row of cabins
where brick-workers once lived
transplanted
along the shore

~

Cherubim
and a flaming sword,
it was written

From then—
exile and mortality

At the entrance
to breezy shores
a thin chain stretched
between posts that hide a motor

~

Of the landlocked
to be suddenly
surrounded by sea
Sun

summoning
past beyond forgetting

~

The cabin feels like an island

Windows unfold to ceiling, floor
uneven, sand collection tower,
jar of shells, afferent breeze

In winter they shut off the water
this place private, seasonal
getaway, sea
still sea

~

Nine day
holiday, time
shared between us, new
grandmother, mother, father,
grandson son

~

Out the screen door
to flowers, fresh cut grass
a low umbrella'd table
two Adirondack chairs
between bushes step
down to a thin stretch of
sand high tide hides, leaves
behind stones, shells, sea

~

Matthew and Peter we've never met.
Among their things:

Toolbox doorstop
Checkered couch
Apricot scrub
Boxes and boxes of Irish Spring
Tristan and Isolde's night-gaze
Tall orange vase emptiness
Bags and bags of frozen vegetables
Mosaic-candle volcano
Kandinsky curtains
Of paintings, Valéry: "The landscape afforded great conveniences"
Lonely sail
Snug straw hat
"Hungary for Men" scrawled on a videotape

~

A. in "the period of likenesses"

Gennady five months dead

But the birches of Yennecott
recall his word-spirits

~

Creeley's Mazatlán
comes to mind, Rez-

nikoff Sei
Shōnagon

across the centuries

I nod
away from my intentions

~

no difference was between the sea and ground,
for all was sea: there was no shore nor landing to be found
(P. O. N.)

~

Awoke in darkness
to the sound of crying

70

then waves

Awoke to her warmth
beside me like sunlight

Awoke not wanting to know
not needing to be

across the sea
on the other shore
of war

~

This place
the Corchaugs called
Yennecott

1876, Town Clerk Albertson
Case tells us
the meaning of this word
is lost

~

Ancient ones
at the principal place
remembered in name
this place their grave
– *nor ghost nor scribe* –

If sea could speak
stars converse
blood return time

dawn sun make
rock flesh
story

then, perhaps

(*chippapuok*)

~

bark walls bullrush mats
and the living place: open sky

~

At the land's tip, a large fence

Anthrax island floats in the water
like a pork chop

(Manittuwond then Plum
stone, Pluym or Pruym plume Patmos)

Operations classified
next to the president's chamber

~

boatyard potsherd dirt
hard as bone, birch
bark Norse, Basque, Breton,
red cloth for fur Thorfinn's
bull, bellows
brake silence
sheep paunch Mi'kmaq launch
Freydis' breasts in turn
delight in vine-stocks, timber, maize
our life and the nine
tripods needed for state
come words
in swords shells
cresthentic cephalothorax
shield sheds shard
green-glazed, lost whole
choice aboriginal name
each boat named
within linked chain

~

sun
down, sea
calm sound
a wealth of boats

appear
people on shore, night
darkens to
silent
rocket-traces

explode
in colors in embers

flaming willow
leaves burst
the sky, fade
to earth

water   ash   memory

~

"The sea we're looking at
always inspires nostalgia
for what we'll never see,"
says Pessoa's maiden
in a round castle-room
with a corpse and a window
and two others, listening

~

sleep surrounded by sea
darkness rocking sleep
beside her in safety

dream
the grain of memory

mythless dream
the shared

impossible dream
dreamless myth impossible

tree without seed, fruit
without flower

～

the build of us
patterns dark the blueing water

(D. J.)

～

Urubamba flow below Vilcapampa
city of stairways in the clouds

The way Castillo's quill trembled
before the undreamed
that was already dreamed

ancient memory

Gandharva realm, keyed
stone carved, angled
vicuña rug, their love
for sun
terrace tillage
harmony of water-
lightness tied
to intihuatana
mirror of bronze

Sun's reflection, echo
of Tiahuanaco

ruins Mayta Capac studied
Pachacutec curved walls

ashlar room window heights
milder than Cusco
hidden by mountains
mist home temple

hidden from conquest

when the merciful conquerors
became the conquered

And the place abandoned imagination

~

Road thru living rock

Land bridge thru the fog

Were we once
two swans in the lake of the mind
until I left to wander

found the city of nine gates
where I lived happily with my wife Purañjani
for many years, then
the city was destroyed and I was reborn
as a woman, married a king and gave birth

to a daughter and seven sons (to this
add the 1100 sons and 110 daughters
of my previous birth)
and while preparing to mount
my husband's funeral pyre
you appeared with the question
as it was written in memory

~

Keel set to breakers
in mapless waters
rather the ice
than their way
Helluland stone
Markland forest
"after Wineland
there is no habitable land
in that ocean, but all that
emerges is icebound, and
wrapped in impenetrable
mist" (Adam of Bremen, 1069)

~

Cabot
blessed by Pope sailed
for King Henry VII, 1497 land-
fall Newfoundland, unseen
latitudes claimed

the same year de Gama
rounded the Cape
of Good Hope
new trade route

Verazzano for France
smelled "the sweetest odors of trees" at sea
First contact: "They are very generous,
giving away whatever they have. We
formed a great friendship with them. . . ."

Portuguese took 57 as slaves,
English kidnapped 3, 1525 Spanish
enslaved 58 [. . .]

Basque *chulpas,* Dutch whalers
furs, fish, oil to Europe
for iron, rum, guns

Settlements formed and failed
Alliances formed divisions
Division formed tribes
PLACE formed NAME

New diseases spread
a new economy

~

Hudson's *Half Moon* spiceless
dream of Cathay
anchors in New Jersey, 1609,
to "very sweet smells" drifting to sea

Claims Delaware Bay to Nova Scotia

Dutch meet the Navasink:
"we durst not trust them"
skirmishes

Cortiaesen hastens beaver slaughter
Argall for English sovereignty
Block lubs
Montauk, *Tiger* burns in Bay:
that when our nation, having lost a ship there
had built a new one, they had supplied them with
victuals and all other necessaries, and
had taken care of them for two winters
till the ship was finished

. . .

Further, they had allowed us to
remain peaceably in their country . . .
we were under obligations to them,
and not they to us

1614 government incorporates the
United New Netherland Company of merchants,
fort built over English protests,
Dutch West India Company merges

mountains of pelts become
mountains of guilders

a commodification of nature to own
deer, water, people

Seal of the new province:
wampum circling beaver

~

Salted meats pipe-staves
pickled oysters for
rum and slaves
tobacco for beaver
otter pelts, Dutch
warred the island
ancestors, massacred,
Kieft tyrant-governor:
Young children, some of them snatched
from their mothers, were cut in pieces
before the eyes of their parents, and the pieces
were thrown into the fire or into the water;
other babes were bound on planks and then
cut through, stabbed and miserably massacred,
so that it would break a heart of stone

No wampum before zeewant

~

There was a before and after
the during consumed

a network of trade at seasons' pace
death and *Kinte Kaeye* the Dance of Death

He was cut to pieces before he could dance
and the other's flesh stripped genitals sliced

two others dragged by a boat and drowned
three more killed while being tied down

Then the pigs were found
to have been stolen by the English

But it was far late, far late
for the indigenous others

~

Second-, third-hand words
make history at best if
firsthand filtered memories

No words left but artifacts
the unfound buried

When the land was a lake
sealed book

:Yennecott

~

Night garden, moon
calendar, soft mint scent.
Warm wind, silent. Gold,
silver debris.

~

The mosquitoes are biting tonight
Like memories

(D. H. L)

~

Caught between Good Hope and Windsor
deer-hide circle scorned
at the mercy of "God" or "nation"

New tributaries formed, new kinships
crossed the Sound, blood-
shed lead peace, to sink

Pequot Sassacus sachem
village burned by Win-
throp English

Mohegan Uncas sachem
marches with Mason
Miantonomi's Narragansett men
join the outer ring

Pequots slaughtered
Confederation splits,
survivors take refuge in
Yennecott

Sassacus
trapped in swamp
escapes to the Mohawks
who send his head to the English

~

Landed on Conscience Point
blind to Sovereignty
behind us and ahead

Promises, waxed valiant in Fight,
and turned to flight the armies of the Aliens.

. . .

The Land of Canaan will I give unto thee
though but few and Strangers in it:

. . .

Thus did the Lord judge among the Heathen,
filling the Place with dead Bodies!

JOHN MASON, 1637

~

One Gardiner in Conetecott
Maſtʳ of works of fortifications
during the English
"war of extermination": *you*
come hithʳ to raiſe thes waſps about my eares,
and then you will take wing and flee away

  . . .

if God ſhould
deliuer vs into thr hands
as Juſtly he may for our ſins

  . . .

Gardiner's thigh
suffered arrowe, buff
Coate preserved
a victorie
to yᵉ glorie of God
& honʳ of our Nation
hauing ſlaine 300 burd thʳ fort &
taken many priſoners

  ~

Of the Pequots, Gardiner writes:
I bid tell them yᵗ they
ſhoud not goe to conetecott for if
they did kill all the men and take
all yᵉ reſt as they ſaid it would doe
them no good, but hurt for Engliſh
women are lazie and cannot doe thʳ
work horſes and Cowes will ſpoyle

84

yor cornefields, and ye hogs th^r clam
banks and So vndoe them

~

One Wyandanch
sachem from Montauk
after the fall of the Pequots
sought trade with Gardiner

What Gardiner wanted:
Pequot heads, five, nine, or twelve
forged friendship

~

In Ludlow's letter to Winthrop,
Ninigret of the Niantic
tells Wyandanch:
"the English are liars
they do it but only to get your wampum"

~

Tide shifts between forks
Yovawam sachem of Pomanocc
(before Wyandanch called sachem of Paumanack)
sells Gardiner Manchonat "the place
where they all died" 1639
three years after Stirling's patent of

Charles I Corp Farrett attorneyed
(Mattouwac Gebroken Land's "first
real estate developer")

Walt Whitman notes as purchased in 1630
for, as the record states,
One large black dog, one gun, a quantity (?)
of powder and shot, some rum, and a few
Dutch blankets

Whitman who in March 1846 calls the slave trade
"a monstrous business . . . a disgrace
and a blot on the character of our republic,"
one year later writes, "With the present slave
states, of course, no human being any where
out from themselves has the least shadow of a right
to interfere," ten years later shifts emphasis,
"In their own country degraded, cruel, almost
bestial, the victims of cruel chiefs, and of bloody
religious rites—lives never secure—no education,
no refinement, no elevation, no political knowledge—
such is the general condition of the African tribes. . . .
the change is not one for the worse, to the victims
of that trade . . . wild, filthy, paganistic—not residents
of a land of light, and bearing their share, to some extent,
in all its civilizations. . . . It is also to be remembered
that no race ever can remain slaves
if they have it in them to become free.
Why do the slave ships go to Africa only?"

~

Among Gardiner's books:
Genevan Bible, *the 3*
Books of Martters, Erasmus, moste
of Perkins, Wilsons Dixtionare, a large
Concordiance, Mayor on the New Tstement

Found his Mordecai
in Wyandanch,
deeds signed

In the end
Wyanadanch poisoned by Tobacus or
Tackapousha or
Corchaugs

awake, awake Ahaſuerous if there
be any of thy ſeed or ſpirit here
and let not haman deſtroy vs
as he hath done our mordecay

~

Myth of the thirteen tribes
Myth of the wedding feast
Myth of the tribe
Myth of the vanishing

Out of Chaldea
into Canaan
thru Tartaria and Scythia
across ice-floe bridge

"the dregs of Adams lost posterity"
"the Devil's offspring"

~

The shore must appear—
Even if there were no shore, it would now have to rise
                    out of the sea

                                        (C. N.)

~

Before Yennecott
before earth was earth
and sky was sky lived
the sky-people (to
the Dakotas water-
people) in the beginning,
words the air

~

How she fell ill beyond cure,
so the elder was sought, said
to uproot a tree and lay her beside
the hole. How the tree

and she broke thru sky-
earth into the endless water
sheet below

～

Two Swans heard the first thunder-
clap, saw sky
break, lifted
her up from the water

～

And the Great Turtle called a council,
said the sky-woman
foreshadowed future good,
asked them to bring some earth from the tree
roots to pack on his back as an island
the woman could live upon

～

The Swans led the animals to the place
where the tree had fallen
Otter, Muskrat, then Beaver dived,
each returned from depths exhausted
and died, others followed
until old lady Toad dove,
breath after breath passed
among the living—all thought Toad was lost
when she surfaced, spat a mouthful of

earth on the Great Turtle's back, and
died

~

The earth grew. Swans circled
the growing earth, and the earth
became the World-
island, rising from the waters on
Turtle's back

~

Within the darkness
the Great Turtle called another gathering
and they decided to put a light in the sky
Little Turtle would climb
the dangerous path up, others
would assist her with magic powers

~

A black cloud was formed full
of rocks clashing lightning
Little Turtle climbed onto
cloud, and while floating around gathered the lightning,
formed one bright ball of light and
threw it into sky, then gathered more for
a smaller ball: the first became the sun,
the second the moon
Great Turtle asked the burrowing animals

to make holes in the sky corners
so sun and moon could descend thru one
and rise thru another, circling
day, night

~

On the ninth day, the sky-
woman gave birth to twins

~

Of Periods of seas—
Unvisited of shores—
                    (E. D.)

~

Ashore, fished
the sound
standing in water

Mosquitos sucked
thru my shirt. Crab after
crab hooked. Moon
a haze of clouds

In the face of hunger

~

1629, Reverend Francis Higginson:
"Thus we see both land and sea abound
with store of blessings for the comfortable
sustenance of man's life in New England."

Buried his daughter
in the Atlanticke, ship's
first death, age four, "many
blue spots upon her breast"
"swayed in the back" "broken and
grew crooked" "the joints
of her hips were loosed and her knees
went crooked" "a most lamentable pain
in her belly and would oftimes cry out in
the day and in her sleep also, 'My Belly!'"
"so that we had cause to take her death
as a blessing from the Lord
to shorten her misery"

After year one, one month, nine days of the
vacuum domicilum, winter killed him.

∼

Puritans divided
under Mosaic spell
sought New
Haven to build
"a refuge for His Noahs and
Lots, a rock," a
"heavenly translation"
spirit driven by crown
and economics

quickly dispelled
chosen ones
with charter

1640 Reverend Youngs settles
Yennecott
church an arsenal, dissenters
like Quakers
fined, whipped, branded,
banished
impure sacrifice

Hutchinson willingly cast
from Boston to Aquedneck
antinomian Congregational
By the voice of His own spirit to my soul

~

When no church meant no
citizenship
and banishment uncertain death
wilderness

trade overseas more greed
expansion,

slavery
altar without sarcophagus

Place bled of ancestral speech
Place bled of ancestors

Cauvin forgotten: *we ought to embrace*
the whole human race without exception
in a single feeling of love; here there is no distinction between
barbarian and Greek, worthy and unworthy, friend and enemy,
since all should be contemplated in God, not in themselves

~

Reverend Youngs believed
in church as state
theocracy wealth
acquired thru real estate

Raised eight children with wife Joan

Only one extant book
from his library:
"the Writings of William Perkins
of Cambridge"

Perkins who breathed his last:
Lord, especially forgive my sins of omission

~

penny royal, laurel, rose-
mary, savin,
flatten this belly
from shame and bondage
spare joy spare pain
replace his seed
with your green

pleasures
pea-
cock flower till
love's readiness, if ever

~

Sarah, Pearsall's "slave for her lifetime,"
"daughter of one Dorkas, an Indian woman"
at age eight sold for sixteen pounds
to Parker and heirs, now their property
"during her natural life": 1698.

~

"If a rooster crowed on your doorstep, company was coming.
If you dropped a fork, it was a man; a knife, a woman; a spoon, a child.
A door hinge creaking was a sign of death.
If the bottom of your feet itched, you were going to walk on strange ground.
If your left ear burned, you would hear bad news; if your right, good news.
If you spilled salt, put some in the fire so as to avoid a quarrel.
Always take salt and a new broom into a house before moving in.
Never cut a baby's nails until a year old or you will make a thief of it."

~

Reverend John Youngs' deed lost, confirmation drawn:

TO ALL PEOPLE TO WHOM THIS PRESENT WRITING SHALL COME, GREET-
ING. KNOW YEE THAT, WHEREAS THE INHABITANTS OF ___, THEIR PRE-
DECESSORS, OR SOME OF THEM, HAVE, IN THE RIGHT AND BEHALF OF THE

SAID INHABITANTS AND TOWNSHIP, PURCHASED, PROCURED AND PAID
FOR, OF THE SACHEMS AND INDIANS OUR ANCESTORS, ALL THAT TRACT
OF LAND SITUATE, LYING AND BEING AT THE EAST WARD END OF LONG
ISLAND, AND BOUNDED WITH THE RIVER CALLED THE ENGLISH TOUNG
THE WEADING KREEK, IN THE INDIAN TOUNG PAUQUACONSUCK, ON
THE WEST TO AND WITH PLUM ISLAND ON THE EAST, TOGETHER WITH
THE ISLAND CALLED PLUM ISLAND, WITH THE SOUND CALLED THE
NORTH SEA ON THE NORTH, AND WITH A RIVER OR ARME OF THE SEA WCH
RUNNETH UP BETWEENE SOUTHAMPTON LAND AND THE AFORE SAID
TRACT OF LAND UNTO A CERTAIN KREEK WHICH FRESH WATER RUN-
NETH INTO YE SOUTH, CALLED IN ENGLISH THE RED KREEK, IN INDIAN
TOYONGE, TOGETHER WITH THE SAID KREEK AND MEADOWS BELONG-
ING THERE TO; AND RUNING IN A STREIGHT LYNE FROM THE HEAD OF
THE AFORE NAMED FRESH WATER TO THE HEAD OF YE SMALL BROOK
THAT RUNNETH INTO THE KREEK CALLED PANQUACONSUCK; AS ALSO
ALL NECKS OF LANDS, MEADOWS, ISLANDS OR BROKEN PIECES OF MEAD-
OWS, RIVERS, KREEKS, WITH TIMBER, WOODLANDS, FISHING, FOWLING,
HUNTING, AND ALL OTHER COMMODITIES WHAT SO EVER UNTO THE SAID
TRACT OF LAND, AND ISLAND BELONGING OR IN ANY WISE APPERTAIN-
ING AS CURCHAUG AND MATTATUCK, AND ALL OTHER TRACTS OF LAND
BY WHAT NAME SOEVER NAMED OR BY WHAT NAME SO EVER CALLED;
AND WHEREAS THE NOW INHABITANTS OF THE AFORE NAMED TOWN OF
SOUTHOLD HAVE GIVEN UNTO US WHOSE NAMES ARE UNDER WRITTEN,
BEING THE TRUE SUCCESSORS OF THE LAWFUL AND TRUE INDIAN OWNERS
AND PROPRIETORS OF ALL THE AFORESAID TRACT OF LAND AND ISLANDS,
FOURTY YARDS OF TRUCKING CLOTH, OR THE WORTH OF THE SAME, THE
RECEIPT WHERE OF AND EVERY PART OF THE SAME WE DOE HEREBY AC-
KNOWLEDGE AND THEREOF ACQUIT AND DISCHARGE THE INHABITANTS,
THEIR HEIRS, SUCCESSORS OR ASSIGNS, AND EVERY OF THEM BY THESE
PRESENTS.

NOW THESE PRESENTS WITNESSETH THAT WEE WHOSE NAMES ARE
UNDER WRITTEN, FOR THE CONSIDERATION AFOREMENTIONED, HATH
GIVEN, GRANTED, REMISED AND CONFIRMED AND DOTH BY THESE PRES-
ENTS GRANT, REMISE AND CONFIRM UNTO CAPTAIN JOHN YOUNGS,

Barnabas Horton, and Thomas Mapes, for and in behalf of the Inhabitants and township of Southold, and for the use of the aforesaid Inhabitants, according to their and every of their sevearl dividends, to have and to hold to them and their heirs forever, by virtue of the afore recited bargain, gifts and grants of what nature or kind soever made with our predecessors, we under written doe confirm all the afore named tract or tracts of land, contained with the afore mentioned bounds, as also Plum island, with waranty against us, our heirs or any of us or them, or any other person, or persons' claime, or from, by or under us, them, or any of us or them, or any of us or them, or any other person or persons, as our, theirs or any of our or their right, title or interest; as witness our hands and seals this seventh of December, 1665, in the Seventeenth yeare of ye reigne of our Soveraigne Lord Charles by the grace of God of England, Scotland, France and Ireland King, defender of the faith &c.

[Signed by Ambuscow, Hammatux and 41 others]
Sealed and delivered in ye presence of us
Benjamin Youngs
Benoni Flint

. . .

Trucking cloth: duffil, coarse wool
named for its origin, Duffel of Belgium

~

And the place
was water
(L. N.)

~

97

Higginson descendent
friend in letters to her
Scholar, Gnome, Wren
she sought
the cold no
fire could cure

The Mind is so near itself—it cannot see, distinctly

Folds of sea, wave-grey
current circulates, touches
crust, recedes

~

Hills full of fish
Coves of shells

Books hidden in bush
under piano
cover

Worm fodder

~

History rock turned word-
illusion, memory the chisel

Contradiction the book of this place
S. H. writes of the new
wilderness

:Yennecott

matters of conquest
name, renamed accident

~

Deep in the Friesland groves
castle Thetingta-State *bosch-lieden*
people of the woods
two Labadists left
by Artemis-crosslight
boarded a small Flute-ship, the Charles,
to tour New Netherland, 1679,
after failure in Surinam
and a year after Anna Maria's passing
she with the heart of Sor Juana
and Sor Juana of her heart
breadth of learning
in twelve tongues
renounced
for *Eukleria*

Concealed in Christ, in the
gown of Elias, white
habit of the Carmelites,
his own elect
seeking new providence

~

Ship full of vermin, passengers
and crew "a wretched set . . . wicked,
impious . . . miserable people"
To eat: spoiled heads of salt fish, dirty
white peas boiled in rotten water,
tainted meat, bread mouldy or wormy

Shark beheaded, brains white as snow
medicine for childbirth
Turkish pirates in the distance

One storm so great
billows as high as mountains
what power, what majesty, what gravity,
order and regularity, what glory, what
grandeur and extensiveness . . . for he permits
such things to come before us in order
that we may see as in a glass who he is . . .
so that we may learn to fear him, and
give him what belongs to him

wrote Danckaerts' in his journal
Wine-racker by trade
with a scientific mind, correcting
charts, mapping the currents, observing
the sea-bottom, stern-
sails for hurricanes

After three-and-a-half months
first contact:
The Indians came on board,
and we looked upon them with wonder.
They are dull of comprehension, slow
of speech, bashful but otherwise bold of

person, and red of skin. They wear something
in front, over the thighs, and a piece of duffels,
like a blanket, around the body. . . . Their
hair hangs down from their heads in strings,
well-smeared with fat, and sometimes
quantities of little beads twisted in it
out of pride. They have thick lips and
thick noses, but not fallen in like
the negroes, heavy eyebrows or eyelids,
brown or black eyes, thick tongues,
and all of them black hair

~

Waters still thick with fish
Sky with birds
More fruit than leaves
Buffalo with deer herds
Hogs asleep stuffed with peaches

in passing through this island we
encountered such a sweet smell in the air
that we stood still, because we did not know
what it was we were meeting

And everywhere "miserable rum . . . *kill-*
devil brandy . . . vile tobacco"

Planters without church or cloister
Sick slaves dug their own graves

One *Najack* home the two travelers
entered: earth floor, roof of reed and chest-

nut bark, posts fastened limbs, roof-ridge
open for smoke, doors at both ends
reed or flat bark, so low one crouched
and squeezed to get in, no lime, stone,
iron or lead, fires at the floor's center,
pot, calabash bowl and spoon, basket
of maize and beans, knife, stone
for tillage, gun with pouch, deer
leather shoes, mats
to sit and lie upon

Canoes without nails, scoops for oars

They walked

as Portugal lost its monopoly on global sugar sales
as gold was discovered in Minas Gerais
and the slave trade tripled:
Know that you are now children of God.
You are leaving for the lands of the Portuguese,
where you will learn the substance of the holy faith.
Think no more of your native lands,
and eat no dogs, rats, or horses. Be happy.

As a century earlier, Spain planned
to conquer China
but only succeeded with pogroms in Manila

~

Danckaert's journal translated in 1867
with "a general account of the Indians"
edited out, the erased not translated
for twelve decades:

"Indeed, the most insolent of our people, as well as many of those with the best knowledge and who do not despise the Indians, as the coarse people commonly do, say that they are all equally dumbfounded by their speech because it is so pregnant with meaning, as we ourselves have noticed; and even those who understand their language fluently have told us many times that they were unable to say certain things in Dutch that were said to them because it was so 'sweet' and full of meaning."

  . . .

". . . because their language is unable to express drunkenness, it is a clear sign that it did not exist among them, for if it had existed there, it would have surely had a name. And with what would they have drunk themselves drunk?"

  . . .

"They also did not have theft because it could also not be expressed; and what would they have stolen from one another?"

  . . .

"Avarice was also unknown to them, because everything was held in common: land, fisheries, hunting grounds; and why would they have stolen or have been greedy, when there was simply nothing to steal?"

  . . .

"Lying and deceit are unknown among them because they cannot say it."

  . . .

"They are, or were, unfamiliar with cursing and swearing, because their language has no words for it."

. . .

"Manslaughter was almost unknown among them, because if you take away greed, drunkenness, deceit and thievery . . . and consider their apparent unconcern about fornication and adultery, then manslaughter has lost most of its power."

. . .

". . . although their language has an abundance of descriptive words and is as rich as one can be."

. . .

"With regard to work, they do nothing at all comparable to labor. Everything they do is a diversion . . ."

~

We were an enigma to all who saw
papist priests or Quakers,
Mennonists, Brownists, David
Jorists, or Jesuists, French spies,
or agents of the Prince of Orange
And thus each one drifted along
according to his wishes

~

Gomarists versus Armenians
to Cocceians versus Voetians
peaked and faded

from the light
Labadie:
"Death is merely ascending from a lower
and narrower chamber to one higher and loftier"

~

Gum
Arabic fused with green
cyclamen leaf buck-
thorn vellum

shellfish tyrian purple lapis
lazuli
        stone
        buried crab claw
emerges scorpion
caterpillar in attic *pious*
diligence

ichneumonidae
disrupts divinity

Sugar colonists
hook, whip, fire
first offense, cut
Achilles tendon,
then a leg

to them
no-name trees greed-
shackle ignorance

Merian
alone with daughter
slaves and paints
"my Indian"

Pineapple thick air, insect
hum, lantern fly
lyre

She notes
the people painted their bodies red
with seeds, patterns "intact for nine
days" before washed away

sailed with her daughter
upriver to the last out-
post La Providence forest
burning sunbeams, fever
heat nearly killed her

Collected lizard pearls
that hatched on ship, tiny
dragons died
at sea

Merian date palm and tulip
anaconda's pull to tree-
top canopy

liver fluke snail
blue morpho imago

~

No other movement save the foundering wreck.

(H. M.)

~

From the ancient base of Piraeus passage
wharves crowded with trade, sea wine-dark

West to the "final stop" of Olson's Pacific, Ahab
"END of individual responsible only to himself'"

Up to the moonlandings, rockets opening prospective
space, secret silo sites below, disgrace, Guantánamo, Bajram

~

Century of church and crown
New Spain
1526 Spanish settle Jamestown

May 18, 1539
de Soto leaves Havana with nine ships
570 soldiers, hundreds of pigs and horses,
Irish greyhounds for "This Governor was
much given to the sport of slaying Indians"
thru Florida and across the South
they marched, always moving, "never
tarrying or settling"
killing thousands, burning them,
throwing them to the greyhounds, kidnapping
many for slaves, women

baptized then raped, villages
destroyed, land ravaged

I have wondered many times at the venturesomeness,
the stubbornness, persistency, or firmness, to use a better
word for the way these baffled conquerors kept on from one
toil to another, and then to another still greater; from one
danger to many others, here losing one companion, there three
and again still more, going from bad to worse without learning
from experience. Oh, wonderful God! that they should have been
so blinded and dazed by a greed so uncertain and by such vain
discourses as Hernando de Soto was able to utter to those deluded soldiers

this Governor, ill governed, taught in the school of Pedrarias de Avila,
in the scattering and wasting of the Indians of Castilla del Oro; a graduate
in the killings of the natives of Nicaragua and canonized in Peru
as a member of the order of Pizarros; and then, after being delivered from
all those paths of Hell, and having come to Spain loaded with gold,
neither a bachelor nor married, knew not how nor was able to rest
without returning to the Indies to shed human blood, not content
with what he had spilled. . . .

Words preserved
with words, embedded
in Oviedo's *Historia*, Ranjel's journal
of his time as de Soto's secretary

From the Bay of the Mother of God,
August 28, 1572,
Brother Juan Rogel writes in a letter:
y que si a de aver algún fruto,
a de ser por discurso de tiempo cavando
en ellos como una gotera en una piedra

108

Smith would echo many years later:
It is more easy to ciuilize them by conquest
then faire meanes; for the one may be had at once,
but their ciuilizing will require a long time and much industry

Amadas and Barlowe sailing for Queen and Raleigh, 1584
beyond landsight
wher we smelt so sweet, and so strong a smel, as if we
had bene in the midst of some delicate garden abounding
with all kinde of odoriferous flowers

First contact: *for a more kinde and loving people there*
can not be found in the worlde, as farre as we have hitherto had triall

Sheriff van der Donck
two years after Youngs settles Yennecott:
It is necessary that we support the planting of a colony,
and the removal of people from the old world, and not a separate
creation, as by the latter the doctrines of the Holy Scriptures
would be subverted and ruined

that after the Christians have multiplied
and the natives have disappeared and melted away,
a memorial of them may be preserved

Traherne, Anglican minister, writing
after the Restoration: *For verily*
there is no savage nation under
the cope of Heaven, that is more absurdly
barbarous than the Christian World

~

Civilian deaths and refugees
in growing millions, war
called casualty, unrest

no glory . . . no glory

left for the living
brokenness, timeless
bitterness

Those here once
as numerous as spears of grass
descendents
on treatied land or without
reinvented in tradition
articulated in smoke

Morning
glory and pine, knowing
transformation

~

Malick's New
World history
cannot hold
its fragrance
of love, the land
even in extremity,
hardship, they belonged
to, communion,
their voices, memory,
of the forest

of the air
of the weeping birds
of the river's stillness

~

Bierstadt's stereoscopic expedition
thru the Nebraska territory,
"We often meet Indians, and they
have always been kindly disposed
to us and we to them. . . ."
His *Rocky Mountain Lander's Peak*
the "consumable landscape,"
foreshortened distances, valleys,
mountains, Bernese Alps, view
reimagined, Shoshone ideal, 1864
staged tableau vivant at the MET
Fair, hired Onondaga impersonators,
spectacle of "imperial subjects"
of the painting, among one
hundred artifacts, Queen's imprimatur,
standing before the scene
today, in the museum gallery,
mountain grass lake bathed
in saintly sunset, figures
of romance concealing
a history of devastation

~

sea
a screen of sun

all-seeing sun of the future past
from which things bloom

zebra grass
tassles wind
spray, osprey

waterway place

qayaq
floats thru
sand-
spit inlet

shore stones worn smooth, green
glass bits, reburied
arrowhead, moon
snail sand collar, skate egg case
empty whelk and mussel shells
scattered bricks

the old man on the island
dock, pulls crabs from traps
and shouts: "It's like
a Cambodian killing field!"

dust motes
in the balance
cormorant archaeopteryx
perched on piling
to wing-dry

sun's calm heart's ease
a word
from the sea, mind's
vacuity

~

Ferried over to the island
across the sound, island
of pristine harbors and fine estates
of workers tending grounds,
at least one suicide, and summer escapes

The Chamber of Commerce map tells us:
"If through some time-machine,
the Manhanssets could return, granted
there would be some culture-shock, but they would
recognize this Island Sheltered by Islands
as the one they knew so many years ago"

~

Here, a butterfly
tickling my sleeve

Ichiyō, dead at twenty-four,
reborn:

"If we search hard enough for the way we will find it"

...

Zhang Ailing says
thru her friend Yanying:
"Every butterfly is the spirit of a dead flower
who has come back in search of itself"

~

Berlin 1921, Joseph
Roth on a walk:
"The inaudible, sleeping
melody of a distant, even
an unreal life"

...

1502, Spain ships the first African slaves to America
1502–1860, more than 9.5 million African slaves are shipped to America

~

the sea withdraws to its deeps
the sea withdraws to its sleep
                              (V. M.)

~

Alone in the woods
near running brooke, far
from wind, shelter built
pyramid of bark
leaves, saplings
provisions set

for the known hour
light deepening late
spring's colors, his eyes
felt but hidden

~

Silence of birds and trees
silence of breath, waves
of pain beginning
silence of walking feet
silence of song
cradling belly
her voice so sweet
sap-rise, soft
bed of moss
butterfly and dragonfly wild
flowers all, root-drink

~

Sun fading, falling thru branches
pain still pain without sin
panis angelius fit panis hominum
as it was as it was
at the sacred table
breath returning
thru the door of horn
vanishes on swift wings
thru the ivory door

~

Cirkell of fiere
embers floating to stars
divine spark inside
breathing   breathing
I am coming, Mesingw
is coming
I am here

~

Beaver appeared, then otter, muskrat,
toad on a lily-lotus, turtle's
slow search earth rocked
tectonic web, spider's net
Mesingw astride deer
face red black mask
eponym of peace, of
silence, steps, breath
making the forest
opening the path
Thoughts born of words:
You are not myself
nor any other
we are: thoughts

~

Surrounded by water and darkness
immersed in the sound of her heart
If this is blindness what is sight?
Before memory

~

They walked toward me from a great distance
and clothed me in garments of sun
faces so familiar, from a city of bridges
city of stone, city of ringroads
waterway fields
now dust motes in a sunbeam
They rubbed my back and my feet
whispered sweet words to me
brought me food and drink
So thirsty I stood
alone
as they danced around me
knowledge and acknowledged
Salt flowing down
my body, a
vessel, my
blood my water
mixing with earth
Horus not of silence or sun
but of the child
The cries in my arms

~

Stepped into water to wash
by dawn's first light
I carried her
she
carried
my heart un-
sequestered forest
Mesingw's breath
everything living emotion
motion in stillness
water clear as the air
was clear, the earth, my
thoughts, hers

~

And after many days
of water-silence, naps
and dreams,
her milk feeding my heart, her voice
gentle wind, her face blossoming sky
I returned to the village of nine houses
without a name, uprooted
not-yet-born calling me calling me
Tears of the Father

Walked the shore of shells
Walked the dock, the glass
Peninsula, the broken pier
Walked the macadam to
Grassy field, walked the path
Thru the trees towering to sand
Walked the mourning dove's nest
In shade and leaves
Walked the templum
Of elfin gold, of orpiment crystals
Tempered with wine
Walked the brickhouse and outhouse
Walked the water back to where
I began
(tho I could see no semblance of a beginning)
And what the walk revealed
Along the sea's margin
Along the rimrock
Of the island
After so many centuries
Of marsh-tides and moonstones
Of or and ore (before oar)
Was an experience of walking
Irony replaced with nothingness
Immensity and transience
The unsaid
Thoughts flowing round my heart
And the rays like a shepherd's fire
Shadowing the vanishing-line

Let us speak of how these perishing
    things
uphold me   so that
    I fall
        into *Place.*

—ROBERT DUNCAN

Bibliographical Note and Acknowledgments

Bibliographies of works sourced in poems are, like civilizations, usually forgotten, lost, or buried with time (usually during the writing-time of the poem).

This seepage of works into work feels as natural as tar bubbling up in a field—sometimes drawn out through seeking, often unconscious or dreamt, always enigmatic, the way words transform souls into words, word bound to word. Into the hearts of listeners the poem transforms as a confluence of sounds! That the evidence a poem bears locates us in the particulars of time and place. This is where the Eternal Body of the imagination begins and ends. Blake's bounding line; the luminous detail. Emerson writes, *To the wise, therefore, a fact is true poetry, and the most beautiful of fables;* Susan Howe calls poetry *factual telepathy;* Comte: *ideal representation of fact;* MacDiarmid: *Wherefore I seek a poetry of facts. Even as / The profound kinship of all living substance / Is made clear by the chemical route;* Jabès: *all the secrets of the universe are buds of fire soon to open;* Stevens: *The poetry of a work of the imagination constantly illustrates the fundamental and endless struggle with fact;* Oppen: *may be said this matter- / of-fact defines // poetry;* or even Frost: *The fact is the sweetest dream that labor knows.* While Louis Zukofsky reminds us: *But to determine the facts does not / mean to give up the struggle;* and H.D.: *No poetic fantasy / but a biological reality, // a fact: I am an entity / like bird, insect, plant.* What can be defined as political or sacred, scientific or philosophical, mythical or quantum mechanical, the poem assimilates and resists, acts upon and resists, is born unto and resists. Its relationship to knowledge and experience is asymptotal as the limits of our understanding shrink and expand—words approximating an ever-evanescent *ou-topos,* or not-place. Poetry looking back and ahead could be said to have preceded the web link as endless connection into world-information, and yet the poem seems anitipodal to such purposes: its means do not sever and isolate the reader from the realm of personal experience, but rather exists through a deepening of experience in the individual being: it seeks a furthering engagement. The poem, which no longer belongs to any particular area of knowledge, is difficult to net—it is already away, somewhere else, rushing ahead on its ongoing encounter with the real. Paul Celan, or Gennady Aygi, has said something to this effect. Dickinson: *True poems flee.* What is the nature of the evidence? There are differences. The desert blooms, maps are made of ruins, walls fall and rise in another desert, revealing an Utes energy experiment of carbon-dioxide-sun-drinking algae. To paraphrase Basil Bunting, not a record of fact but the truth of the poem, *that is of another kind.*

Of his author notes "written in the margins" to *A Tree Within,* Octavio Paz says: "Poems are born from a circumstance and yet, as soon as they are born, they free themselves and take on a life of their own. In poetry the mystery of human freedom unfolds: accidents, circumstance, are transformed into a work. For this reason, notes are expendable." For "notes" read "bibliographies."

With this in mind, in gratitude and thanks, I note here a few sources that are induction ballast to this book. For "Yennecott," John A. Strong's *The Algonquian Peoples of Long Island From Earliest Times to 1700* (Heart of the Lakes Publishing, 2000) figured as inspiration and content, more so than some of the encyclopedic histories of the island, like Ross's or Thompson's. Other documents, texts, and exhibit-sources referred are embedded in specific sections of the poem, like Danckaerts' journal—which is among the earliest reliable written accounts of the American indigenous that survive—and the lines of other poets that are always guide and treasured company. Susan Howe's sublime *Souls of the Labadie Tract* is the thread that lead me to the Labadists and on to Danckaert and Henry C. Murphy's 1867 incomplete translation of Danckaert's journal. Charles Gehring and Robert S.

Grumet translated the missing section in their 1987 article "Observations of the Indians from Jasper Danckaerts's Journal, 1679–1680."

"Tide Table" is based on the William Kentridge film installation of the same name. His *thinking aloud* (Verlag der Buchhandlung Walther König, Köln, 2006) also seeped into the poem.

The epigraph to "Throne" is translated by Michael A. Sells and is from his book of pre-Islamic odes, *Desert Tracings*. Archaeologist John Malcom Russell's two books *Sennacharib's "Palace without Rival" at Nineveh* (University of Chicago Press, 1992) and *From Nineveh to New York* (Yale University Press/Metropolitan Museum, 1997) played a similar role as Strong's in this poem.

A sentence Russell said in an interview is stuck to the wall above my desk: "There is something about having a past, having a sense of who you are that allows you to measure yourself against what political leaders or market forces think you should be." And

> how deep the past
> is poetry
> as young as old

Jeffrey Yang is the author of two poetry books, *Vanishing-Line* and *An Aquarium*, winner of the PEN/Osterweil Award. He is the translator of Su Shi's *East Slope* and *June Fourth Elegies* by 2010 Nobel Peace Prize winner Liu Xiaobo. Yang works as an editor for New Directions Publishing, and lives in Beacon, New York.

Book design by Connie Kuhnz. Composition by BookMobile Design and Publishing Services, Minneapolis, Minnesota. Manufactured by Versa Press on acid-free 30 percent postconsumer wastepaper.